1970s DIESELS AND ELE

A Steam Enthusiast Looks Back

Copyright Book Law Publications 2011

ISBN 978-1-907094-29-3

FOREWORD

The title of this book could be considered an oxymoron because I make no bones about it: I am a steam man through and through. With British Railways' steam declining in the mid-1960s I got so disgusted with how it was being allowed to die without dignity that I started to go abroad more frequently where there was still steam aplenty and generally, well looked after. But at most, that could be for no more than 4 weeks a year which left 48, so when steam did eventually finish on BR, I more or less went into a 48-week hibernation!

Then in mid-1972 my employer moved me from London to Bristol, where my life would change in so many ways, apart from railway. On arrival I quickly reacquainted myself with two fellow enthusiasts that I had met and befriended on different steam tours of Germany. They were The Honourable James (Jim) Cadman, of Bath – sadly no longer with us – and Terry Nicholls, a life-long railwayman, now retired, who still lives in Bristol. Those two gentlemen made me feel very much at home in my new surroundings and quickly convinced me that I should "get out a bit more" and take another look at Britain's railways. We were certainly a mixed trio, with widely differing backgrounds, but over the ensuing years Jim and Terry would become my companions on visits to the few industrial railways still using steam, to the UK's fledgling preserved railways and on several very memorable trips overseas.

Then Terry particularly, suggested that we should look more at the British Railways scene where even first-generation diesels were under threat and much steam-age paraphernalia still clung to a precarious existence. So over the time up to October 1978, when I moved abroad to live for more than eleven years, I amassed a collection of pictures, some of which I now present in this book. I make no apology for the South of England and former GWR lines' bias, but these are very personal pictures for me in that they are reminders of two very special friends and the great times we had together.

Therefore, I respectfully dedicate this book to Jim Cadman, so sadly missed, and Terry Nicholls, the railwayman and superb photographer, for the years of friendship and the travels we made together.

Roger Griffiths, Cyprus, 2011

(Cover picture) **See Page 17**

(previous page) **By the time I moved to Bristol the D800 type was nearly finished and reduced to working on mundane duties. In August 1972, 814 *DRAGON*, already shorn of nameplates, trundles past the newly-opened station at Bristol Parkway with a Class 8 freight, a lowly duty indeed! The combination of a setting sun and my one and only experiment with GevaColour film, has given the loco the appearance of having a purple livery. 814 had been withdrawn in January 1972, only to be reinstated four months later. The stay of execution was brief though as the locomotive was finally taken out of service just three months after I took this picture.**

Printed and bound by The Amadeus Press, Cleckheaton, West Yorkshire

First published in the United Kingdom by Book Law Publications, 382 Carlton Hill, Nottingham, NG4 1JA

DIESEL-HYDRAULIC TYPES - For the Great Western Railway, there was only one way of doing things: the Great Western way! So it was, with the first years of BR Western Region - or should I say, (Great) Western Region? The region specified diesel-hydraulic types for its new fleet, whereas the rest of BR went down the diesel-electric path. The WR's decision had merit in that it did not want to reinvent the wheel as it were, but use tried and tested, but alternative, technology. So they based their original diesels on the V200 Bo-Bo of Germany's Deutsche Bundesbahn, which employed a stressed-skin body as opposed to heavy metal frames and side plating, and lightweight, high-speed diesel engines and hydraulic transmissions instead of heavy marine-type engines, electric generators and traction motors. The result was that with the D800 class, BR (WR) got 2000hp in an 80 ton loco on four axles, whereas the contemporary English Electric Type 4, also of 2000hp, weighed-in at 133 tons, carried on eight axles. To the WR's Traffic people those 53 tons saved represented another carriage or two that could be hauled, carrying more paying passengers. All the better then, to more quickly pay off the investment in the new motive power. Or so it was thought! By the beginning of the 1970s, BR's management considered that the WR's locomotives were not "corporate" and were, so-say, more expensive to maintain. So the diesel-hydraulics were consigned to an early demise, something very much regretted by some enthusiasts, especially those living in former GWR-land!

Diesel-hydraulic 818 *GLORY* is seen in splendid condition as it stands by the turntable at Swindon works, in May 1975. D818 emerged from Swindon in March 1960 and was withdrawn in November 1972. Later it provided parts for preserved sister 832 then became the cosmetically-restored hulk placed as seen, as a tribute to the locomotive works. 818 was cut up in November 1985, five months before closure of Swindon works.

An "in-yer-face" shot of 825 *INTREPID* (also no nameplates) from July 1972, shows just how badly the B-B had been allowed to deteriorate – hardly a good advertisement to the travelling public! 825 was hauling a Class 6 freight through Bristol Temple Meads station, to leave its train at Bristol West before retiring to Bath Road diesel depot. Another short term return to traffic had allowed me to capture this scene as 825 had been withdrawn in January 1972, with reinstatement in May. Who knows though, this picture might have been of 825's last duty, as it was withdrawn in August 1972.

Another diesel-hydraulic type under threat when I got to Bristol, was the Hymek, 101 of which had been built by Beyer-Peacock, 1961-1964. I hated those 1700hp, B-B engines with a passion, for it was they in particular that wrote finis to my beloved GWR *Castles*! Here (D)7022 stands at Bristol Bath Road depot in August 1973, while over the garden wall as it were, Brush Type 4 No.1602 looks on. Although 7022 was one of the last four of her class to be withdrawn, in March 1975, she would be outlived by no less than 30 years by Brush 1602. That loco would be renumbered 47474 in February 1974 and later carry the name *SIR ROWLAND HILL*, before being withdrawn and scrapped at the end of 2005.

Hymek diesel-hydraulic (D)7037 basks in the sun outside the former steam repair shop at Old Oak Common depot, in November 1971. In the distance can be seen Western 1052 *WESTERN VICEROY*, which would outlive 7037 by thirty seven months. The Hymek was withdrawn in September 1972, with 1052 following her to the scrap yard in October 1975. The steam repair shop has recently been demolished to make way for a station, as part of London's Cross Rail project.

The most impressive and undoubtedly most popular class of diesel-hydraulic were the Westerns, 74 of which emerged from Swindon and – horrors! – Crewe works during 1961-1964. The 2700hp C-C type weighed just 108 tons, again continuing the WR's striving for a high power-to-weight ratio. But, the type could not be converted to Electric Train Heating as was becoming standard in BR's coaching fleet and this, added to their being non-standard and "costly" to maintain, saw the Westerns disappear by early 1977. In the summer of 1976 there were a few Saturday trains for the Paddington - West of England route still rostered for the remaining Western class locomotives and they were accordingly much photographed! Here 1048 *WESTERN LADY* speeds her 8-coach train down Bruton Bank, headed for Plymouth and beyond. Built at Crewe in December 1962, the diesel would continue in service until February 1977, to be preserved and pass into the care today, of the Midland Diesel Group at Ripley, Derbyshire. Of further historical comment, note the telegraph poles still in use, and the fact that the picture was taken from the abutment of the erstwhile bridge carrying the Somerset & Dorset line over the GWR.

Another duty that came the way of the Westerns in their final years was the St.Blazey china clay trains and return empties. In a June 1976 picture that is full of history, 1023 *WESTERN FUSILIER* comes out of Whiteball tunnel and over the summit, with clay empties. Note the banker-holding siding behind 1023 and the crossover in the foreground that in steam days would be very busy, slotting banking engines in between heavy passenger traffic, for the banker's return to Wellington station and its next assistant duty. Whiteball signal box is just out of picture to the right and it controlled the crossover and semaphore signals. The white panel painted on the retaining wall of the tunnel to highlight that distantly-seen signal, is still visible today, though somewhat faded. 1023 was withdrawn in February 1977 and is preserved as part of the National Collection, at York Museum.

Once again, a lowly duty for a Western, in May 1973, as 1042 *WESTERN PRINCESS* hauls train 2B68, consisting of two unidentified broken-down locomotives. The Western is taking a Brush Type 4 and English Electric D400 from Westbury, for repair at Bristol Bath Road depot. The trio is seen approaching Bradford Junction on the Westbury – Bath line, having just passed beneath the aqueduct carrying the Kennet & Avon canal over the railway. 1042 would be withdrawn just two months later.

DC ELECTRIC TYPES - The Wath – Sheffield – Manchester via Woodhead, line was heavily graded and heavily trafficked – mostly with coal from Derbyshire to the northwest. Following experience with the North Eastern Railway's Shildon electrification scheme (1915 – 1935), the LNER made a start on the electrification of the Woodhead route, even to the building of the first Class EM1 locomotive, which left Doncaster works in 1941. However, World War Two put a stop to further works so it was left to British Railways to finish the scheme, which came into full operation in 1954. The voltage used was 1500 DC, based upon considered best practice at the time, after considerable earlier use by the railways of France and Holland. To run the full service over the route, 57 more Class EM1 Bo-Bo, of 1868hp, were built for freight work, together with 7 Class EM2 Co-Co of 2490hp, for fast passenger services. Some electric multiple units (EMU) were also built to carry suburban traffic. As is well known, it was not long after the Woodhead route was electrified that BR decided the future standard for electrification schemes would be 25kv AC. Declining traffic saw the EM2s withdrawn in 1968 when they were stored in the old steam engine shed at Bury, before being bought for further service in Holland, in September 1969. One EM2 was cannibalised for spares leaving her six sisters to work on Dutch railways until withdrawal in 1986. This left the EM1 class to soldier on, but with the Woodhead route's overhead infrastructure coming due for renewal, BR decided that it was too expensive so the section between Penistone and Hadfield closed in July 1981, when all remaining EM1 were withdrawn.

The Woodhead route electric locomotives were housed and serviced in two depots, one at each end of the line. That at the eastern end was located alongside the marshalling yard at Wath upon Dearne and this November 1972 picture shows E26018 standing at that depot. The BR TOPS scheme listed the EM1 as Class 76, so E26018 was duly renumbered 76018, and then in June 1976 the Bo-Bo was renumbered again, this time to 76035. Withdrawal came with closure of the route in July 1981.

Normal practice for freight haulage over Woodhead was for double-headed EM1 on loaded trains with a single unit on empties or light loads. In both directions the line climbed through dramatic scenery, especially on the eastbound grade, where by extreme coincidence we see 76035 (*see opposite*) passing the dam of Torside reservoir in May 1977. The water in the reservoir is recovering from the empty state reached during Britain's scorcher of a summer in 1976.

Bound for Hadfield, a three-car EMU comes off Dinting viaduct on 1st August 1978, crossing over to take the branch line to Glossop. There it will reverse and return to Dinting, then continue up the main line on the short run to Hadfield. Under TOPS this type of unit became Class 506, of which eight, 3-car sets were built in 1954 for the Manchester – Glossop – Hadfield service. That ran at half-hourly intervals during the week, on a round trip that took ninety minutes. Therefore with one unit in reserve and another away at works at any one time, there was no spare capacity for the Class 506 to run other services. On rare occasions they did venture beyond Hadfield, but this was unusual because of the units' low gearing and propensity for the motors to overheat. Eight Motor Open Brake Seconds and eight Trailer Open Second (built as Trailer Composite but declassified in 1960), were built by Metropolitan-Cammell, with the remaining eight Driving Trailer Open Second coaches coming from Birmingham Railway Carriage & Wagon. The units continued in service until 1984 when the Manchester – Hadfield section was converted to 25kv AC.

As remarked above there were two depots serving the Woodhead route with the primary maintenance centre being at Reddish in Manchester, where it was situated alongside the Fallowfield Loop line, and opened in 1954. In its latter years Reddish depot also serviced and maintained diesel-electric locomotives and this continued until 1983 when the depot closed to subsequently be demolished. Sundays at Reddish used to see considerable numbers of EM1/Class 76 parked up for the weekend on the depot's west side, as here on 1st May 1978. Note how it was usual practice for parked DC locomotives to keep their pantographs raised, as against the AC types where they were lowered when not in use.. 76028 (E26028) is the nearest locomotive; it would continue to work until July 1981 and closure of the Woodhead route.

A view inside Reddish depot's two-road servicing shed on 1st May 1978 reveals the usual detritus of an engine shed: an oil tank, gas bottle, tools and a ladder lying on the ground, the brake blocks and their hangers. 76011 and 76008, the latter still quite spruce after rail tour duty, accompany the last-built of the DC EMUs. That EMU is interesting in that it is a reminder of a very old railway practice – the staff train. The Woodhead route was built by a predecessor of the Great Central Railway and the GCR was a regular employer of special trains that picked up locomotive depot staff from a central location and carried them out to what was usually, a remotely-situated depot. Such trains were often known as "Didos" and one in particular that lasted into BR times was that serving the former GCR engine shed at Annesley, north of Nottingham. The two Class 76 seen here, would be withdrawn in July 1981.

The End is approaching! 1st May 1978 and the remains of 76050 are seen by Reddish depot's east side stabling roads. The locomotive was withdrawn in February 1977 and shorn of its bogies for spares, thus presenting a sad sight. Formerly E26038, then 76038 and 76050 from November 1976, the locomotive's body would languish until February 1984, when it was scrapped in situ by Messrs C.F.Booth, of Rotherham. An English Electric Type 4 perhaps looks on and considers it own fate......

The Southern Region of BR provided itself with some electric locomotives for hauling freight and heavy trains like the London - Paris Night Express. To provide greater flexibility, the E5000 electric locos were rebuilt to incorporate a diesel engine that allowed them to work over non-electrified lines. The resulting TOPS Class 74 were, however, not a success, so they were withdrawn after a few years. However, the E6000 class was built as an electro-diesel hybrid from the start, having 1600hp when working as an electric loco and 600hp as a diesel. What became TOPS Class 73 must be considered a success as some are still in use with sector operators as this is written. The clock at Bournemouth Central station was not working, so it is later than indicated, on the evening of 11 October 1977, as electro-diesel 73135 (E6042) marshals parcels vans, prior to hauling them to London. It is believed that 73135 still exists today as part of the South West Trains' fleet, but stored, out of use.

In May 1976, Electro-diesel 73128 (E6035) needs all of its 600 diesel horsepower to lift a heavy coal train from Old Oak Common East, to North Pole Junction on the West London Joint line, and onwards via Kensington Olympia to Clapham Junction. So, light on haulage power then, but also light on braking capacity it seems. Note the two Diesel Brake Tenders positioned between 73128 and its train, to give additional stopping capability. Diesel nostalgia then, but this picture is full of so much more for your scribe. In the distance a Brush Type 4 passes under a footbridge as it trundles into Old Oak Common depot. On Saturdays in steam days that footbridge, which led from the Grand Union canal towpath, could have fifty or more train spotters watching the constant action on the Paddington main line and the busy comings and goings from Old Oak's engine and carriage sheds. See where once many Pannier tanks barked back and forth, the Brush Type 2 on carriage duties, with its paintwork all washed out from too many passages through the carriage washing plant! And the two line side boxes – one of them green – where Old Oak Common East Signal Box used to stand, with its constant bell codes drifting across to us on the footbridge. Withdrawn in February 2002, loco 73128 survives today on the Pontypool & Blaenavon Railway, but that footbridge is long gone, as is the Brush Type 2 and probably its Type 4 sister. And Old Oak Common, once one of London's premier locomotive sheds, is closed, with its site to be utilised as part of the new CrossRail Project.

DIESEL-ELECTRIC TYPES - Upon Nationalisation, BR inherited some 20,000 steam locomotives of a bewildering range of types, of which many were very old, having survived only through the exigencies of World War 2. So quite sensibly, BR decided to rid itself of as many "oldies" as soon as possible and replace them with a fleet of Standard steam locomotive types that were envisaged to last until the end of the 20th century. So much for plans! Indeed, some Standard locomotives were built, but the rapidity of their replacement by diesel and electric traction saw most of them go to the scrap yard after just a few years service – a considerable waste of public money! So what did BR do when it ordered new diesels? As discussed, the Western Region went its own, and therefore, expensive way, but instead of BR purchasing a standard fleet for the other regions, they bought numerous different diesel-electric designs from various manufacturers. With the exception of one or two types – the Brush Type 2 comes to mind – the first generation fleet were a mediocre to poor purchase at best – look at the dreadful Metro-Vick Bo-Co! In other words, yet another waste of public funds. Even then, after only a short while, reducing and changing traffic patterns rendered most of the lower-powered machines redundant, while BR's most powerful diesels had little better performance than the steam locomotives they replaced. So there came an expensive, second generation of more powerful machines, but a Britain of rapidly changing travel habits ensured that even they did not have lives long enough to justify their costs. In your scribe's opinion, not an auspicious venture!

A 'phone call from Terry Nicholls one Saturday morning in October 1972, suggested I join him at Bristol Bath Road depot where (D)400 had just arrived, on reallocation from the Midland Region. In the autumn sunlight 400 stands alongside a Peak and Hymek (D)7050, with stabled on the same track, still in green livery but with double arrow logo, is Brush Type 2 (D)5838. Eventually, all of 400s sisters would come to the Western Region to replace the fading diesel-hydraulics. 400 would become 50050 and receive the name *Fearless* in August 1978, to be withdrawn in March 1994. She was not scrapped, however, and is today preserved at the Yeovil Railway Centre. 7050 was just one month from withdrawal, while 5838 would become 31305 and survive until November 1991.

Healey Mills marshalling yard was a busy place in the early 1970s with constant comings and goings of freight traffic. A good spot to watch some of this activity was at the junction just south of Horbury and Ossett station and during a few hours there in November 1972, I saw among other things, this green English Electric Type 4. I recall that (D)239 was twittering away quite industriously as it headed south with a heavy train of coal hoppers, probably bound for Ferrybridge Power Station. This loco received its TOPS number of 40039 in February 1974, but was destined never to be repainted in BR blue as it was one of the first five of its type to be withdrawn, in January 1976.

19

I well remember seeing my first BR Modernisation Plan diesel – D600 *ARK ROYAL* - at Paddington, late in 1957. The second to come my way was a couple of months later when I was spotting at Stonebridge, northwest London, where the Euston main line crosses the North Circular Road. The friendly signalman in the goods yard box called out "there's a new diesel coming" and trundling along came D8000, to be based at Britain's first diesel depot, the adapted steam shed (1D) at Devons Road, Bow. Little did I realise then, what those two early diesel locomotives were the start of! The D8000, or English Electric Type 1 was one of the more successful of BR's first generation machines and eventually grew to 228 in number and become TOPS Class 20. Still in green livery, but renumbered from D8169 in February 1974, 20169 is seen at Tinsley in April 1976 coupled as a twin unit, to a blue-painted sister. 20169 was withdrawn in December 1995 and is preserved at Kirkby Stephen East station.

Another first-generation type was the Sulzer Type 2, a Bo-Bo of 1160hp. The trouble with the design was that it had to lug around its own 79 ton weight before it pulled any train, so it was not really powerful enough. Nevertheless, 151 were built and are represented here by 24037 (D5037) at Northwich in March 1976. Note the folding, Southern Region-style indicator discs, which were a legacy of its initial allocation to that Region. Also that when built the locomotives were fitted with nose-doors for multiple working but these have been plated over. Despite looking in reasonable condition, 24037 was just four months away from withdrawal.

The **Class 25**, also known as Sulzer Type 2 when built, were an improvement on the machine seen in the previous illustration, in that they had a 1250hp engine and were geared for 90mph working against the "too-slow" maximum of 75mph, of the Class 24. Early Class 25 models, such as (D)5169, still in green livery at Tinsley in November 1972, retained the nose doors and some had no train heating boiler fitted – as noted by the "NB" on the cab side. 327 of the type were built during the period from 1961 to 1967 and 5169 would become 25019, receive a blue livery and be withdrawn in September 1980.

A big surprise at Taunton, on 14th August 1976, was 25211 and 25069 double-heading the 0949 Nottingham-Paignton service, with the driver unashamedly "grandstanding" for the assembled public, with lots of Sulzer "chat"! See the detail differences in the later Class 25 in that no front doors had been fitted, which allowed a deeper centre windscreen. 25069 (D5219) was withdrawn in December 1983, while 25211 (D7561) would survive until July 1986.

Having most of its network electrified, the Southern Region had less of a need for diesel locomotives but specified their own particular requirements, resulting in the 98 machines of the Birmingham Railway Carriage and Wagon (BRCW) Type 3, of 1550hp. Later they would become Class 33 and many enthusiasts would refer to them as "Cromptons" because of their Crompton-Parkinson electrical equipment. Returning from a business meeting on 13 October 1977, I impulsively called in at the closed Semley station on the former LSWR main line from Waterloo to Exeter. In that route's sadly reduced state of the time, Class 33 locomotives were handling a service of semi-fast passenger trains between London and Exeter. My visit happened to coincide with 33024 passing through with just such a working. Note the sadly decaying remains of the station with, surprisingly, an intact canopy and the telegraph pole route still in use. Delivered in 1961 as D6542, the locomotive would be withdrawn for scrapping in February 1986.

Working flat-out, an unidentified BRCW Type 3 hauls its train up the 1 in 37 grade of the Exeter St. Davids to Exeter Central line, in April 1976. This was a mandatory place for spotting and photography in steam days with Bulleid Pacifics and Class N slogging up the hill with one or more Class E1/R 0-6-2T tanks pushing at the rear, a banking duty that would pass, in the late 1950s, to Class Z 0-8-0T. In the distance, at St.Davids station, a Peak can just be seen as it lays-over on the site of the former GWR steam shed (83C). Note also the building at right, with roof ridge vent. That was a venerable, Bristol & Exeter Railway-built carriage shed, then some 130 years old.

And now for something completely different! Locomotive 1200 *FALCON* sits beside Bristol Bath Road locomotive depot in March 1973. Built as a private venture by Brush of Loughborough as a prototype for a possible second-generation fleet, the diesel entered service in September 1961, originally numbered D0280. It differed from previous diesels in that it was fitted with two Maybach MD655 engines, *a la* the WR's Westerns, but instead of hydraulic transmission it employed Brush generator and traction motors. D0280 worked first from Finsbury Park depot on East Coast main line workings, which also included a stint of St.Pancras – Sheffield trials, but its Maybach engines were unfamiliar to the staff at Finsbury Park, so the locomotive was sensibly moved to Bristol, where it worked alongside the Westerns. D0280 remained the property of Brush until its sale to BR in 1970 when it received the number 1200 and was destined to become TOPS Class 53, but this was never effected. This was because its non-standard status condemned 1200 to an early demise and it was withdrawn in October 1975, to be broken up by Messrs Cashmores of Newport, in March 1976.

On a beautifully sunny day, 23 May 1976, I joined many other enthusiasts at Foxfield, Cumbria, waiting for B1 Class 4-6-0, 1306 *MAYFLOWER* and A3 Class 4-6-2, 4472 *FLYING SCOTSMAN*, to pass by with a special train from Carnforth to Ravenglass. All that could be heard was the sound of distant sheep and some skylarks overhead, when there came, from the direction of Ravenglass, another sort of twittering - that of the English Electric Type 4. And then they appeared: two locomotives, 40001 and 40098, both working, but with only a single full brake in tow. Quite what this working could have been was a puzzle, but it made an interesting little interlude before the double-headed steam arrived! 40001 (D201) would be withdrawn in April 1984, while her younger sister (D298) would precede 40001 to the scrap yard by exactly three years.

What became the standard Type 4 diesel on BR, the Brush Type 4 appeared in 1962 and featured a 2750hp power unit in a 113 ton body, a considerable improvement in power to weight ratio over earlier diesel-electric designs. Eventually 512 of the class would be built and become TOPS Class 47. First allocations to the Western Region were in the mid-1960s, presaging the end of the diesel-hydraulics. (D)1932 went new, to Bristol Bath Road depot (then still coded 82A) in February 1966; that locomotive is seen here in April 1973 leaving Twerton Tunnel, Bath with a Paddington-Bristol express. 1932 would become 47493 in May 1974, then 47701 in January 1979, when it also received the first of three names: *ST.ANDREW*, followed by *OLD OAK COMMON TRACTION & ROLLING STOCK DEPOT* (August 1991) and *WAVERLEY* (May 1997). The Co-Co would work for Network Southeast, RES and Fragonset, before being stored at M.o.D Ludgershall in February 2007. Eventually withdrawn the locomotive was privately preserved and can be found today at the Dartmoor Railway, Okehampton.

Northbound at Stafford on 28th April 1978, Brush Type 4 Co-Co 47199 (ex D1849) passes with empty Merry-Go-Round coal hoppers from Rugeley power station to Silverdale Colliery. The mainstay of the LMR power station coal hauling operation, these particular Class 47s were fitted with slow speed control (SSC) which enabled them to creep very slowly beneath the colliery loaders and then over the power station discharge points. Note the steam-age London Midland Region maroon, station name boards still in place.

29

Immingham depot's 47184 approaches Old Oak Common East, in May 1976, having just left the West London Joint line at North Pole Junction; where the train was bound for is not known. Many memories again here: the distant gasholders, with an approaching DMU passing under the Ladbroke Grove flyover, built to ease the passage of empty coaching stock to the departure side of Paddington Station. The WLJ over bridge – Mitre Bridge - across which in steam days, used to pass a steady procession of south – north London freights and a few passengers - usually troop trains - headed by locos from Feltham and Hither Green depots. And, I could have had no idea that 18 years later, where I stood would be covered by the North Pole Eurostar depot, now itself no longer in use. Loco 47184 had a complex history! Delivered new as D1779, to Tinsley in October 1964, it would become 47184 in February 1974 and then in January 1981 be renumbered again, to 47585, upon allocation to Bristol. A third renumbering would occur in January 1994, to 47757. Three names would be carried: *COUNTY OF CAMBRIDGESHIRE* (May 1979 - December 1990); *RESTITUTION* (April 1994 - ?) and *CAPABILITY BROWN* (March 2003 – September 2005 [withdrawal]).

On a lovely late afternoon in September 1976 47239 is captured on film leaving Merehead quarry with a Yeoman stone train bound for London. The line in the foreground leads to the quarry while that on which the train is travelling was the former East Somerset branch which ran from the Berks & Hants main line at Witham, through Shepton Mallet, to Yatton, on the Bristol – Taunton main line. The route closed in 1969 leaving just the Witham – Cranmore stub for access to Merehead. Like the Brush Type 4 described in the previous caption, 47239 had a long history with three number changes in its life after delivery in November 1965 as D1916. It became 47239 in April 1974, 47657 in July 1986 and 47812 in August 1989. The locomotive would be named *PRIDE OF EASTLEIGH* in February 2002 but would carry those plates for only eighteen months. After a period with Freightliner the diesel moved to Riviera Trains for whom it still works today, based at Crewe, and restored to its original two-tone green livery.

More Somerset stone traffic for a Brush Type 4, with 47055 just catching a break in the clouds on 12th April 1978. The locomotive is hauling stone empties at Sherrington, on the Wylye Valley line between Salisbury and Westbury. At Westbury 47055 will run round its train and haul it west to either Whatley quarry (off the Frome line), or to Merehead. Here again is a long life story for what was D1639, delivered in December 1964. The Brush became 47055 in May 1974, then 47652 in April 1986, to change again, to 47807 in July 1989. It would be named *THE LION OF VIENNA* in April 1998, and carry those plates until July 2002. Even that was not the end though as the diesel became 57304 in September 2002 and received the name *THUNDERBIRDS GORDON TRACY* in October the same year. 57304 is still in service with the Thunderbird fleet, based at Longsight, Manchester. (*For information contained in the previous four captions, the author acknowledges the vast store of knowledge to be found at the website:* www.class47.co.uk)

May 1975 found me at Swindon, so I decided to get a picture of a train passing the famous locomotive works. On reflection I could have chosen a cleaner locomotive than Class 50 No.50048 but the moment passed and circumstances did not give me the chance to go back there. 50048 (D448) would receive the name *DAUNTLESS* (for HMS Dauntless) in March 1978. In fact the name Dauntless has been carried to sea by five ships of the Royal Navy, since 1804 - the latest of which is the ultra-modern Type 45 destroyer, commissioned in June 2010. The Class 50 *DAUNTLESS* would carry that name until being withdrawn for scrapping in July 1991.

Early morning, 17 January 1978 and Terry Nicholls telephoned to say: "it's been snowing on the Berks & Hants and now the sun is shining. Come on"! So off we went to arrive at Lavington in superb lighting conditions, with the bluest of skies. We made our number with the "Bobby" in Lavington signal box, who made us a nice cup of tea while we waited for the first train. It was 50013, going hard at it with a West of England express that passed with a cheery toot and wave from the driver. 50013 (D413) would be named *AGINCOURT* three months later and carry the plates until withdrawal in March 1988. There had been five HMS Agincourt since 1796, the fourth of which was a super-dreadnought that fought at the 1916 Battle of Jutland and was unique in that she was the only battleship ever to mount her main armament in *seven* turrets, each of which had two 12-inch guns.

And so to the 'Deltics'. Here was another class I loathed because of their part in the demise of the East Coast Pacifics, so I never photographed them when I lived in London. However, by May 1975, I decided that perhaps I should, so a rare visit to London saw me at King's Cross to meet a friend. While waiting I took this picture of Deltic 55018 *BALLYMOSS* waiting for departure with its train for Newcastle, while an unidentified Brush Type 4 approaches Platform 8. By the mouth of Gasworks tunnel 40075 performs the time-honoured duty of stand-by locomotive, while behind the small group of platform-end spotters, another Deltic can just be seen inside the small servicing shed. 40075 (D275) would be withdrawn in December 1981, two months after 55018 (D9018). So many memories of steam here 1950 - 1963! Locomotives slipping merrily away on the sharp curves of the servicing point; 0-6-2T slogging out of the tunnel from the Widened Lines, and tenders, some of them with corridor connections, slowly backing out of Gasworks tunnel with much anticipation: would it be a rare Haymarket Pacific? When it was, the elation that was felt!

THE WEYMOUTH TRAMWAY - The Weymouth Tramway was opened by the Great Western Railway in 1865 running mostly through the town's streets, to carry goods and passengers (from 1889), from the station to the port, for the Channel Islands ferries. Goods traffic ceased in 1972 and passenger trains in 1987; the last known use of the line was on 2nd May 1999, when, using a combination of 37250, 73106 and 73138, two trains ran from Yeovil Junction. Today the line is owned by Weymouth & Portland Borough Council which proposes to remove it when funds become available. Jim, Terry and I paid a visit to Weymouth on 30th July 1977, to record the passage of that day's Channel Islands boat train, which was hauled by 33105. It was high summer and Weymouth was crowded, so there was much dealing with traffic and some shenanigans with parked cars, despite yellow lines being painted on road surfaces everywhere! 33105 (D6517) was one of twelve members of the class that were specially built with narrow bodies, to allow them to work over the width-restricted Tonbridge – Hastings line. The locomotive was withdrawn in October 1987.

The train had left the station area with the obligatory pair of pilotmen holding the traffic at the various crossroads to allow passage of the boat train. By now slightly better progress is made along the quayside, with much squealing of wheel flanges on the check-railed, sharply curved line. Some vintage cars here: A Ford Capri and Cortina Mark 1, an Austin Cambridge and Mini, while on the right can be seen a Rover 2000, a Volvo 144? and the ubiquitous white Transit van!

Just squeezing between a Cortina Mark 2 and a Ford Granada at left, which had just been "bumped" out of the way(!), 33105 and train approach the ferry terminal. Tastefully attired in a lilac shirt, Terry Nicholls strides ahead to get his next picture. Note the warning bell and flashing orange light on the front of the locomotive.

DIESEL DEPOTS AND STABLING POINTS - As stated earlier, when BR was formed it inherited some 20,000 steam locomotives. They were based at almost 700 engine sheds, buildings that ranged from a tiny lean-to, barely able to cover the smallest tank engine, through to massive structures with multiple turntables under one roof and capable of housing over 100 locomotives. As steam declined so too did those sheds, but BR still needed depots in which to stable and tend to its new diesels and electrics. So, depending upon the Region and its available financing, the late-1950s onwards saw some brand-new depots being built and a number of steam sheds adapted, in varying degrees, to house the New Order. Or, a steam shed would be demolished but diesels (usually) then were parked on the site and men signed on and off for their duties. Most of such places are now history, but today's multiplicity of railway operators sometimes provide themselves with small depots for their own locomotives.

A wet night in November 1972 at 82A, Bristol Bath Road depot, with Brush Type 4 (D)1593 standing outside the six-road shed while a DMU, Peak and a 350hp shunter are warm and dry inside. The depot had been custom-built in 1960, on the site of a 1932, ten-road GWR shed, that had itself replaced a six-road Bristol & Exeter Railway broad gauge depot and the former B&E works that in the late 1870s, had been converted by the GWR to a twin-turntable shed. So a lot of engine shed history here – alas no longer. Bath Road diesel depot closed in May 1995 and was eventually demolished to make way for a 5000-seat arena and entertainment centre. But that has not materialised because of lack of funding so the entire site remains depressingly derelict. Brush 1593 became 47467 in 1974 and would be withdrawn in January 1999.

The 1854 two-road steam shed at Warrington (Arpley) – a BR sub-shed of 8B, Warrington (Dallam) – was closed in May 1963, to quickly be demolished and allow diesels to stable on the site. A visit there in April 1976 found eight locomotives: a Brush Type 4, two Sulzer Type 2, two 350hp shunters and three English Electric Type 4. Nearest the camera, 40115 and 47214 can be identified. The first, (D315) would be withdrawn in March 1982, while in typical Brush Type 4 fashion, 47214 would have a history! Delivered in May 1965 as D1864, the Co-Co was renumbered to 47214 in February 1974, keeping that number until withdrawal in December 1994. Three names would be carried: *ANTAEUS* (May 1982 - ?); *TINSLEY TRACTION DEPOT* (September 1987 – December 1989); *DISTILLERS MG* (November 1990 – June 1993).

The former GWR three-road shed at Swansea East Dock (87D), was built in 1893 and closed in June 1964. It was quickly removed but diesel locomotives did not stable exactly on the site; instead they were parked a short distance away on what had been the outer shed yard. When visited on a Sunday in June 1975, five English Electric Type 3 were found, each coupled to a brake van in readiness for Monday's return to work. 37253 is nearest the camera: built as D6953 the Co-Co would be renumbered twice, first in February 1974 and again, to 37699, in December 1985. Withdrawal took place in August 1997.

AC ELECTRIC TYPES - Just as with diesel locomotive types, when BR went shopping for the first AC electrics they ordered what was basically, the same overall design – so some notion of standardisation! – but in five sub-types, AL1 – AL5, from different manufacturers. The result once again, was less than a success, either economically or operationally. Three of the sub-types would require considerable attention and then rebuilding to try and improve their performance, a course of action that met with only limited success and led to some early withdrawals. However, based upon the greater success of the main sub-type, the AL5, came the better AL6 and later, the even better AL7. Those machines saw out the 1970s to be followed by other classes, but the Sectorised future of Britain's AC lines lay with multiple units for passenger services, and some diesels for freight, so today sees much fewer electric locomotives in use.

The last visit I made to a modern traction depot, before my move overseas, was on 25th June 1978, which found me at Willesden, not far from where I grew up. This interior shot shows three types of AC locomotive: 3200hp AL1 81002 (E3003), was designed by British Thompson Houston and twenty-five were built by Birmingham Railway Carriage & Wagon Company. They were troublesome and underwent some rebuilding, ending their days on Euston empty carriage workings. 81002 was withdrawn in October 1990, but is today preserved by the AC Electric Group at Barrow Hill engine shed. Pretty much the same can be said for 3300hp AL2 82003 (E3049), which was one of ten built by Beyer-Peacock to a design by Metropolitan-Vickers and was withdrawn as early as July 1983. The AL6 class will be described in a later caption, but just to add that 86039 (E3153), would be renumbered 86639 and remains in use today with the Freightliner fleet.

41

3100hp Class AL4 84004 (E3039), has just emerged from Crewe Works in December 1975 after a second rebuilding. Despite that the locomotive would be withdrawn in November 1977. Ten AL4 were built by the North British Locomotive Company (NBL) to a design by General Electric. Despite being one of the world's premier builders of steam locomotives for well over one hundred years, NBL found itself unable to successfully enter the modern arena of diesel and electric traction. To illustrate: all AC locomotives employ rectifiers to convert the 25kv AC overhead line current to 750v DC for the traction motors. Despite the existence of early-design solid state rectifiers, NBL used Mercury Arc rectifiers, a technology dating back to 1902 and when employed in the demanding surroundings of a locomotive, they were a serious and constant source of trouble. So much so that all the AL4s spent two periods of being in store, along with Class AL3, in the old steam shed at Bury. But traffic demands meant that BR had to spend a lot of money trying to keep them in service – all to little avail. Despite being such an ill-starred design, 84001 is today preserved as part of the National Collection, because it is the only surviving post-steam, main line locomotive built by NBL. Such a sad tribute to what was one of Britain's greatest exporting companies!

Stafford station on 28th April 1978, as loco 85038 brings its train of British Oxygen tankers to a halt at signals. The train was being held so that the Brush Type 4-hauled passenger train, seen in the distance, could pass and proceed in the direction of Crewe. Forty of the 3200hp Class AL5 were built at Doncaster Works 1961-1964. Their comparative success led to the design of the AL6, following the introduction of which the AL5 were mostly to be found on freight traffic. 85038 (E3093) would continue in service until being withdrawn in January 1990. With the exception of four units, the entire class was cut up by MC Metals, of Glasgow. Note the remnants of another era: the steam-age porter's hand trolley and barrow casually left standing on the platform. What future employment would it find?

Rare, on a passenger working, AL1 No.81008 heads a train of Mk.1 coaches forming the 1545 Birmingham-Manchester, through Stafford on 28 April 1978. The loco came into service in October 1960 as E3010 and after some problems and attention from BR, withdrawl came in March 1988, with scrapping over three years later, at the Sheffield yard of Messrs. Coopers Metals.

AL6 86204 rests between duties at Basford Hall sidings, Crewe, in May 1975. One hundred of the type were built by BR's Doncaster works (forty) and English Electric's Vulcan Foundry (sixty), entering service in 1965/6. Depending upon the traction motors fitted, the AL6 came in three different power versions, 3600hp, 4040hp and 5000hp and they dominated services on the West Coast main line for many years. 86204 was built as E3173 and is of interest because it was the test-bed for the flexi-coil suspension seen on the side of the locomotive. This was because as built, the AL6 were damaging the track under high speed working with the so-called 'hammer-blow' effect. So when the enhanced springing tests with E3173 proved successful in solving the problem, the modification was added to the rest of the class. Of other note is that between the years 1978 and 1998, 86204 carried the name *CITY OF CARLISLE*, latterly working for Virgin Railways. The Bo-Bo was withdrawn in August 1998, but lingered until July 2003 before being scrapped at Immingham Railfreight terminal. Of 86204's sisters, some are still in use with Freightliner, some are stored at M.o.D Long Marston, waiting a very dubious future, and four were even exported to Hungary for use by one of that country's private operators.

A resplendent 5000hp, AL7 No.87004 stands in Willesden electric depot on 25th June 1978. Built four years earlier at Crewe works, 87004 was to have been numbered E3204 but this was never carried. However, the entire class soon received names, with 87004 becoming *BRITANNIA*, which had formerly been carried by the doyen 'Britannia' class BR Standard Pacific. The AL7 would remain in service until introduction of the 'Pendolino' multiple units when they would either be withdrawn, or sold on to other users. In fact, an expression of interest came from, of all places, Bulgaria and in time no fewer than seventeen of the thirty-six AL7 would be exported there. Withdrawn in June 2005, 87004 was among them, moving overseas in November 2009 with a new number: 87004-8, to be employed by a private operator, the Bulgaria Railway Company.

DIESEL SHUNTING TYPES - Among the myriad of steam locomotives inherited by BR were thousands of small types used solely for shunting wagons and carriages in the many yards around the country. With the end of steam, small diesel locomotives had to be produced to take over such shunting duties and for short-distance trip working. The pre-Nationalisation companies had all introduced small numbers of shunting diesel locomotives of about 350hp, before the Second World War and BR continued with that theme in large numbers. These were mostly diesel-electric 0-6-0s, but a fleet of smaller machines, was also introduced, of 0-6-0 or 0-4-0 wheelbases and usually of mechanical transmission, but there was one type with diesel-hydraulic drive. As traffic dwindled and wagon-load freight became a thing of the past the shunters were left with little to do so most have disappeared. However, a few remain in service with various of today's railway operators and on preserved railways.

Slumbering in the sun at Bournemouth Central on 11th October 1977 and perhaps, providing useful 'weathering' detail for the modeller, is the Class 09 derivation of the standard 08. The 09s were fitted with higher ratio gears which enabled a top speed of 27½ m.p.h. making them suitable for trip working and pick-up freights. The higher gearing was specified by the Southern Region and all sixteen of the type went to that Region initially. Because of their extra 'usefulness' perhaps, every Class 09 is still in existence, some privately preserved and some still in everyday railway service. 09026 (D4114) is one of the latter and is today based at Brighton, Lovers Walk depot where it acts as the depot shunter and also in the unique role (for a shunter), as a track de-icer, but that particular task only within the depot limits.

A total of 3150hp is seen in this line of nine of BR's standard 350hp 0-6-0 shunting locos, which were TOPS classified 08. They are taking a weekend break at Newport, Monmouthshire in November 1972, but present a decidedly non-standard appearance. Four are still in green livery while the other five, in BR blue, feature three with the BR 'double-arrow' logo on the engine compartment, whereas the other two have cab side logos, such differences being due to the local conditions at individual locomotive repair workshops.

Typical of the smaller shunting type mentioned before is 0-6-0 diesel-mechanical D2089, seen at Bradford Hammerton Street (56G) depot in November 1972. Powered by a 204hp Gardner engine with a Wilson-Drewry gearbox, 230 of this type would come from Swindon and Doncaster workshops during the period from 1957 to 1961. Note that the locomotive has a radiator blind fitted, ready for a Yorkshire winter, and at rear, is a permanently attached 4-wheel flat wagon. This was from an idea originated on the Great Western Railway with its familiar 'shunters' trucks', and meant, apart from carrying shunters (as in men) about, to give the locomotive a long enough wheel base to ensure that track-circuiting was always bridged. D2089 would become TOPS-numbered 03089 and be withdrawn in November 1987, the last of its class to work at its then base of Norwich, but it still exists, in working order, on the Mangapps Farm Railway.

All through the history of Britain's railways, non-traffic departments, like engineers, signals, sleeper depots, carriage and wagon works etc, were supplied with their own motive power for internal use. This continued into BR times and the diesel era as evinced here by 0-6-0 diesel-electric PWM651 (Permanent Way Machine), seen at Radyr Civil Engineer's yard on the Western Region, in March 1975. Ordered in 1959 from Ruston and Hornsby and fitted with a Ruston 165hp engine and British Thompson Houston generator and traction motor, the loco and her four sisters worked from various Departmental yards around the Western Region. They eventually lost the initial green livery in favour of Civil Engineering yellow and later, PWM651 would be TOPS-numbered 97651. The locomotive remained in use to about 2005 and is today preserved, far away from the Western Region, on the Strathspey Railway, at Aviemore.

DIESEL MULTIPLE UNITS (DMU) - To replace scrapped steam locos on branch line, suburban, cross-country and some inter-city routes, BR introduced a first generation of many different styles and manufacture of DMU, ranging from small four-wheel railbuses, to single, twin, triple and quadruple units. Except for a couple of models with hydraulic transmission all of the many hundreds built used mechanical transmission, via automatic gearboxes and most had control gear that allowed different types to be worked in multiple. The DMUs can be said to have revolutionised rail travel in Britain until line closures and the all-conquering motor car caused passengers to forsake rail. Today a few first-generation units are still in use by operators for revenue-earning services and in a departmental role; many are preserved on Britain's heritage railways.

Bearing all the tell-tale signs of 38 years old Agfa Colour's fading emulsions, is this picture from August 1973. I apologise for the lesser quality of the illustration, but have included it because of the wealth of steam-age infrastructure it includes. Derby-built three car DMU, B (for Bristol) 407 has just left Frome and is crossing Blatchbridge Junction to regain the Berks & Hants main line to go to Castle Cary and then via Dorchester to its destination, Weymouth. But what else can be seen? The very fully-equipped telegraph poles, the semaphore signal and the little shunt signal in the shadow of the DMU and of course, Blatchbridge Junction signal box itself. Then there are the two speed-restriction signs telling drivers not to exceed 50 m.p.h. if taking the left hand route to Frome, or 80 m.p.h., if going right, along the 1933-built Frome cut-off line. Lastly, a quarter-mile post tells us that we are 116¾ miles from Paddington. There is one item of modernity to be seen, apart from the train, and that is the flange-greaser that also can be detected in the front shadow of the train.

Morning sunlight and shadow at Sheffield Midland station in November 1972 as a three car DMU pauses on its journey to Hull. Built by Metropolitan-Cammell, the unit displays that maker's characteristic front end and aluminium window surrounds. The type would be TOPS classified 101 and see a long life, with the first examples entering service in 1956 and the last being withdrawn from public use in 2003.

By the mid-1970s many first-generation DMUs were getting 'tired' so instead of expensive replacement, BR embarked upon a programme of refurbishment, giving the renovated machines a distinctive new livery. For comparison with the illustration opposite, here from February 1977, is another Metro-Cammell three-car DMU, seen at Doncaster, on its way to Manchester and displaying the 'refurbishment' paint scheme. In the event the refurbishment only put off the necessity for BR to introduce a fleet of new DMU types, but with finance still very short, the result was the awful 'Pacer' and 'Sprinter' types, none of them anywhere near as comfortable as the first-generation diesel multiple units. Such is progress!

Once again displaying its independent spirit, the Western Region of BR specified single-car diesel units, following on from the precedent set by the GWR's diesel railcars of the 1930s. Eventually they would become the TOPS Class 121 and be nicknamed "Bubble cars" by enthusiasts. That nickname was used in the marketing of present-day operator Chiltern Railways, which still uses a couple of the units on the Aylesbury – Princes Risborough service. In a nostalgic picture for your scribe, a single car Class 121 has just branched off the Bristol – Filton main line at Narroways Junction, headed for Avonmouth and Severn Beach. A lot has changed since this scene was captured in August 1976. The double track section at far left has long been lifted and above the train can be seen a set of sidings that were serving a scrap yard, the products of which were taken away by rail; that too has gone. On the other side of the main line can be seen some cylindrical tanks, once part of a large gasworks; the site is now an industrial estate. Then in the distance is a tall chimney – also now gone – below which is Lawrence Hill station – still open!

HIGH-SPEED TRAINS (HST) - By the early 1970s BR had decided that it needed a new fleet of high-speed trains, but not having the finance for large-scale electrification projects, had to go for diesel power, after a flirtation with gas turbines had proved unsatisfactory. This entailed high-revving diesels to maintain a constant power output and as light an axle load as possible. A prototype was built at Crewe in 1972, a rake of carriages with a power-car (locomotive) at both ends, each using Paxman Valenta engines of 2500hp and weighing 70 tons. Given a DMU class number of 252, it came into use on timetabled services in May 1975, between Paddington, Bristol and Weston-super-Mare and proved the concept, with the result that the order to proceed was given, with introduction of the trains planned for 1976.

Another railwayman friend of mine arranged a visit to Crewe Works in December 1975, to see the new trains under construction, but the first sight we saw was of one of the prototype's power-cars, its job now done and waiting a decision about its future. Sensibly, with such an important development in British railway history, the unit was saved and now rests in the National Railway Museum at York. Further into the works we came upon these power car front ends being fabricated in the erecting shop, ready to be attached to the bodies, one of which can be seen in the right background. One has to wonder why, when the whole front end would be finished in yellow, BR did not get all the components delivered in that colour!

The very first HST power car is nearing completion, waiting for the Paxman engine to be lowered through the roof and the body finally prepared for its new, dedicated livery. When we tried to find out what that livery would be, we were told it was very secret and would be seen at the 'launch' of the new trains! Note that the production model power car lacked the buffers provided on the prototype, but a drawbar has been fitted, normally hidden behind a cowling, for shunting and rescue purposes. Service HST sets would receive classifications of 253 and 254 and I could never have envisaged that these machines would be the last ever new locomotives to be constructed at the mighty Crewe works!

My first encounter with an HST came in May 1976 when I was line-siding opposite Old Oak Common carriage sidings, where I captured this close-up of 253025 and the very distinctive corporate livery first applied to the HST fleet. The Inter-City 125s had arrived and like the first-generation DMUs they would revolutionise British rail travel. The full HST express passenger timetable came into use on the Western Region in June 1977, which displaced the incumbent Brush Type 4 and English Electric D400 types, they being cascaded down to cross-country, slower speed passenger, sleeper trains and suchlike.

The next picture I took of an HST was in November 1976 and through an incredible coincidence, it too featured 253025! The train is seen in the very pleasant surroundings of Sydney Gardens, Bath, with a Paddington – Bristol service. The driver looks as if he's just been ordered: "stick-em-up"! Actually the bright, low morning sun was obviously causing vision problems as he was fiddling with the sun visor.

SIGNALS - In my foreword I said that one of the reasons I "got out a bit more" was to capture the remnants of the steam age. In the West of England we were fortunate in that semaphore signalling remained in use until fairly late so some of the diesel pictures I took purposefully included mechanical signals.

Some rare occurrences here at Westbury in May 1975, where apart from the marvellous but threatened signal gantries, we see an unidentified Peak hauling a scarce parcels train of four vehicles. The train had just passed through the station and is signalled to go straight ahead to Fairwood Junction, where it would join the Berks & Hants main line and on, westwards. The Peak itself was unusual for Westbury, its presence occasioned by closure of the Bristol – Taunton line for engineering work, with consequent diversion of traffic via Bath, Bradford-upon-Avon and Westbury.

A bright, but grey sky helps to silhouette the superb signal gantry that once stood at the west end of Taunton station. It is seen here in April 1976, as 50025 accelerates from the station slack, on its way to Plymouth. 50025 (D425) would be named *INVINCIBLE* in June 1978, a name carried by seven Royal Navy warships, the last being the aircraft carrier that saw action in the Falklands War. Her predecessor was a First World War battlecruiser that saw successful actions at the battles of Heligoland Bight and Falklands (appropriately) before being lost at the 1916 Battle of Jutland, with just six of her crew of 1032 men surviving the huge explosion. Locomotive 425 was also a little ill-starred, being withdrawn, due to accident damage, in August 1989.

And now for history, that isn't quite! No guessing where this is as we visit Blackpool North station in September 1976, to see the array of platform starter signals. Not quite history because at the time of writing this terminus is the largest station in Britain still controlled by mechanical signalling. Alas you are not likely to see so many excursion trains nowadays with two, English Electric Type 4 waiting with their trains for the day-trippers to return, happy and full of fish and chips and Blackpool Rock! In the distance, two DMUs can also be seen, the one on the right being Derby-built units while the one on the left looks like it may have been a product of the Birmingham Railway Carriage & Wagon Company. Notice too that although the station's eight platforms are equipped with electric lighting standards, a venerable gas light – then still in working order – may be seen just left of centre.

The December 1975 sun is just setting at Exeter as 50016 (D416) pulls away from its station stop, en route for Plymouth. It is passing a lovely set of Up line signals and on the bridge over the River Exe, Terry Nicholls is once again 'getting in on the act', capturing a classic 'going-away' shot by framing the train with the signal gantry. 50016 received the name *BARHAM* in April 1978. That name was last carried by the ill-fated Queen Elizabeth class battleship, sunk by U331 in the Mediterranean on 25th November 1941, with the terrible loss of 862 souls. The locomotive *BARHAM* would be withdrawn in August 1990.

RAIL TOURS - In the closing days of BR steam, hundreds of special train were run for enthusiasts – known by BR in its Working Time Tables as "CRANK EX", for Crank Extra, which shows what BR really thought! So it was with diesel traction that when a class of locomotive was dwindling, the number of special trains using them ramped up. Later of course came that strange breed (strange to me that is – no offence!) called the "Traction Bashers", but they had not really emerged in the 1970s.

So here are a few of those diesel specials, starting with the '*Hymek Swansong*' of 22nd September 1973, which took the following route: Paddington - Swindon - Severn Tunnel Junction - Maindee North Junction - Pontypool Road - Abergavenny - Hereford - Worcester - Oxford – Paddington. The trains was hauled by 7001 and 7028 (what a pity they were not the 'Castles' formerly bearing those numbers!), and apparently a speed of 96 m.p.h. was attained at Steventon on the outward journey! The pair is seen here at Patchway, just about to enter the Severn tunnel. The 'Swansong' title was not quite accurate because although 7001 was withdrawn in March 1974, 7028 was one of the last four Hymeks withdrawn, in January 1975.

The low winter morning sun of 13th November 1976 backlights 47120 as it pulls out of Bristol Temple Meads station with 'The Severn Valley Limited' comprised of the magnificently restored SVR train of ex-GWR coaches. Alas such wonderfully nostalgic stock is not allowed to run on BR nowadays as the Health & Safety Gestapo says it is unsafe – even though it ran problem-free, for many years under the GWR and early BR! 47120 left the Brush works at Loughborough in January 1964 numbered D1709, to be given 47120 in March 1974. The locomotive was a relatively early casualty, being stored in December 1990 and withdrawn March 1994. Two names were carried: *R.A.F. KINLOSS* (June 1985 – September 1987); *OSPREY* (unofficially at Tinsley, September 1989 – storage).

A class of locomotive that attracted a huge amount of attention as it approached extinction was the 'Western' (Class 52) diesel-hydraulic. Many tours were run, but a potentially interesting one was RPPR's *Western Requiem* of 20th February 1977. I say 'potentially' because the plan to use a 'Western' in several Welsh valleys did not quite come off. Locomotive 1010 *WESTERN CAMPAIGNER* got from Paddington to Cardiff alright, but then had to 'retire hurt' to Canton depot. The very hasty replacement was an unfortunately grubby Class 37 No.37179, which handled the Cardiff – Pontypridd - Treherbert – Pontypridd – Aberdare – Pontypridd sections of the trip. Meanwhile, with commendable flexibility and speed, 1023 *WESTERN FUSILIER* was summoned from far-away Old Oak Common and moved quickly enough to meet the tour at Pontypridd as it returned from Aberdare. This picture shows 37179 returning from Treherbert and passing the lovely Taff Vale Railway signal box at Gyfeillon, on the approach to Pontypridd.

In this illustration we see Pontypridd Junction signal Box, with 37179 running in past a just-arrived *WESTERN FUSILIER*. Look at all those trespassing enthusiasts! If the meddlesome Health & Safety busybodies had been around in those days, they would have been having kittens by the litter! 1023, took the train from Pontypridd to Merthyr, then via Cardiff Queen Street and Central to Filton, Bristol Doctor Days Junction, Bath and Swindon to Paddington.

RPPR was a prolific promoter of diesel-hauled rail tours in the 1970s (where are they now?) and its '*Silver Jubilee*' trip brought a pair of Brush Type 2 to the West Country on 14th May 1977 with 31414 and 31416 in charge. A second RPPR rail tour, featuring a pair of Brush Type 2 came west on 22nd October of that year, with the wonderful name of '*Toffeeapple Farewell*' No it was not saying goodbye to sugar-covered fruit, but to the original batch of twenty Brush Type 2s, apparently known as 'Toffeeapples'. The route followed by 31005 and 31019 was ambitious in that it took in branch and freight lines around Bristol, as follows: Paddington - Reading - Newbury - Hawkeridge Junction - Bath - Bristol Temple Meads - Portishead ('Peak' 46039 assisting to allow run-round) - Bristol Temple Meads - Montpelier - Avonmouth - Filton - Westerleigh Junction - Yate - Tytherington - Yate - Bristol Parkway - Doctor Days Junction - Bath - Swindon – Paddington. The two locomotives were superbly turned out by their home depot, Stratford, with that shed's 'signature' white roofs – even down to white-painted wheel rims! The pair is seen here approaching Tytherington Quarry on the former Yate – Thornbury branch, where the run-round was made difficult by some dodgy track – but luck held! Again the term; Farewell' was a bit premature as 31005 (D5505) survived until February 1980, while sister 31019 (D5519) existed for a further eight months.

Yet another RPPR tour brought a Deltic to Wales – the '*Deltic Dragon*', on a bitterly cold Sunday 29th January 1978, 55018 *BALLYMOSS* ran Paddington - Didcot - Oxford - Evesham - Ashchurch - Cheltenham - Gloucester - Chepstow - Severn Tunnel Junction - Newport - Cardiff Central, where English Electric Type 1s 20030 and 20142 ran Cardiff - Radyr - Pontypridd - Treherbert and return. 55018 then ran Cardiff - Severn Tunnel Junction - Chepstow - Gloucester - Stroud - Swindon - Paddington. A family occasion meant that I had to miss the Deltic and only see the train on its run to Treherbert behind the pair of EE Type 1. Here 20030 and 20142 are proceeding along the valley of the River Rhondda and have just passed Lewis Merthyr Colliery with the once-ubiquitous rows of Welsh miners' cottages on the hillside. The colliery ceased production in June 1983 and is now the centre of a wonderful visitor attraction, the Rhondda Heritage Park. Of the two locomotives, 20142 (D8142) is also 'heritage', in that following withdrawal in February 1992 it was privately preserved and as D8142, is today housed at the London Underground's West Ruislip depot. 20030 (D8030) was withdrawn in October 1990 and scrapped.

A very complex 'Gwent Valley Invader' tour was run by F & W Railtours on 11th March 1978, involving the following:: EE Type 4, 40120 running Crewe - Alsager - Stoke-on-Trent – Uttoxeter - Derby - Burton-on-Trent - Tamworth - Water Orton - Birmingham New Street - Bromsgrove - Droitwich Spa - Worcester - Cheltenham - Gloucester - Chepstow - Newport. Then Type 3s 37269 and 37233 ran Newport - Aberbeeg - Waunllwyd (Ebbw Vale) Newport - Maindee North Junction - Llantarnam Junction - Blaenavon and return to Newport. Brush 47001 substituted for a failed 40120, Newport - Bristol Parkway - Westerleigh Junction - Yate – Cheltenham -Birmingham New Street, where EE Type 4 No.40044 took over and ran: Derby – Uttoxeter - Stoke – Crewe. Time again precluded much personal activity so I got just a single picture, of 37233 and 37269 running south from Aberbeeg, having just passed the remains of Llanhileth Colliery. Just about where the tail of the train is, Llanhileth Junction signal box once stood, from where a branch used to pass to the right of the fence seen in the foreground, climbing steeply to Crumlin High Level. The train will soon pass the sites of Crumlin Low Level station and the once-mighty, Crumlin viaduct. 37233 (D6933) was withdrawn in June 1999, whereas 37269 (D6969) would become 37417 and survive with Direct Rail Services, until about 2010.

Here is a fitting picture with which to end this album. 26th February 1977 and came the time to finally write *finis* to the Westerns, as BR ran the '*Western Tribute*' rail tour, using 1013 *WESTERN RANGER* and 1023 *WESTERN FUSILIER*. The train took a route that included most of the 'Western's' old haunts: Paddington - Swindon - Newport - Cardiff - Swansea - Filton Junction - Bristol Temple Meads - Plymouth - Taunton - Westbury - Reading – Paddington. The sun was getting low by the time the train got to Bristol, where a large crowd had gathered to see its passing, as '50' 50037 waited for the rail tour to precede it westwards. Both 'Westerns' were withdrawn two days later, but 1013 went into the care of the Western Locomotive Association while 1023 joined the National Collection at York. 50037 would not survive. After being named *ILLUSTRIOUS* in June 1978 the locomotive was withdrawn in September 1991 for scrapping.